Sheep Laughs

How do Jewish sheep celebrate their coming of age?
With a baa-mitzvah?

How do Spanish sheep greet each other at Christmas?
"Fleece navidad!"

What is a sheep's favourite Bible story?
Joseph and his Technicolor Dream Goat.

N⊘T
THE PARABLE
OF THE
LOST
SHEEP

Other books by the author

The Lost Parables Series
The Donkey and the King
Ana and the Prince
The Princess and the Crocodile

Not the Bible Titles
Not the Parables of Jesus
More Not the Parables of Jesus
Not the Parable of the Good Samaritan
Still More Not the Parables of Jesus
Not the Parable of the Lost Sheep (free for subscribers)
Not the Parable of the Rich Fool (subscribers only)
Not the Christmas Story Vol 1 (with devotional)

Christian Parody Titles
Not the Love Dare
Not the Christmas Story: A Comedic Christmas Caper

Christian Satirical News
The Best of the Salty Cee Vol 1

Satirical Publishing Titles
Get 1,000 Readers for Your Self-Published Book

N⊘T
THE PARABLE
OF THE
LOST
SHEEP

REVISED SATIRICAL VERSION (RSV)

John Spencer

Not the Parable of the Lost Sheep
Copyright © 2019 John Spencer.

All rights reserved. No part of this book may be copied or reprinted for commercial gain. However, these stories are meant to be shared, used as skits, sermon illustrations, stories for Sunday school or for small group discussion. Individual parables may be reproduced for these purposes, but please honour the effort that went into writing them by referencing their source. For other uses please obtain written permission from the author via his website www.johnspencerwrites.com.

Unless otherwise quoted, all "Not the Bible" quotations are taken from the Revised Satirical Version (RSV) © 2017.

Nothing in this book is intended as a substitute for the Bible. The reader should regularly consult a Bible in matters relating to his/her spiritual development and particularly with respect to any behaviour that may require truth.

This is the part of the copyright page where I write something funny for those readers who have OCD. But let's face it – that last sentence wasn't at all funny.

Published by:

Kingdom Collective Publishing

Unit 10936, PO Box 6945
London, W1A 6US
kingdomcollectivepublishing@gmail.com

Book and Cover idea by John Spencer, design by Akira007
Not the Bible icon – design by John Spencer, created by Dalmatirac Design Studio
Editing by Katherine.
ISBN: 978-1-912045-88-4

First Edition: August 2019

Get this book for Free!

You can get the ebook or audiobook version of this book free by subscribing to my mailing list at:

www.johnspencerwrites.com/signup

If you stick around, you'll also receive "*Not the Parable of the Rich Fool*". Twenty satirical takes on this parable not available anywhere else.

In addition you'll also receive:

- an email every Friday chock full of the week's memes I put out on social media
- details of the monthly competitions where you can win free signed copies of my books
- notifications of all promotional deals on my books
- opportunities to beta read and receive free review copies
- other freebies I issue from time to time
- the satisfaction of making John feel loved and wanted.

CONTENTS

SHEEP LAUGHS ... 1
GET THIS BOOK FOR FREE! ... 7

THE ORIGINAL PARABLE ... 9
LUKE 10:1-7 ... 11

NOT THE PARABLES ... 13
VERSIONS 1-25 ... 15

PERFECT PARABLES ... 41
VERSION 26 ... 43

POINTLESS PARABLES ... 45
VERSIONS 27-33 ... 47

PUNNY PARABLES ... 55
VERSION 34 ... 57

THE LOST PARABLES ... 59
THE PARABLE OF THE PARAPLEGICS AND THE RACE ... 61

NOT THE BEGINNING ... 65
FEEDBACK ... 67
GET BONUS CONTENT ... 68
KEEP IN TOUCH ... 69
OTHER BOOKS BY THE AUTHOR ... 70
ABOUT THE AUTHOR ... 72

The Original Parable

Just in case you forgot...

Not the Parable of the Lost Sheep

Luke 10:1-7

Now the tax collectors and other notorious sinners were all drawing near to hear Jesus, but the Pharisees and the scribes complained, saying, "This man welcomes sinners and eats with them."

So Jesus told them this parable:

"Suppose one of you has a hundred sheep and loses one of them. Wouldn't he leave the ninety-nine in the open country and go after the one that is lost until he finds it?

"And when he finds it, he will joyfully carry it home on his shoulders. When he arrives, he calls together his friends and neighbours saying, 'Rejoice with me, for I have found my sheep that was lost!'

"In the same way, there is more joy in heaven over one sinner who repents than over ninety-nine righteous people who need no repentance."

Not the Parable of the Lost Sheep

NOT the Parables

Different takes on the parables to restore the wonder, the joy of the Gospel and the discomfort of discovering what we really believe in our hearts.

Not the Parable of the Lost Sheep

1

Now the tax collectors and other notorious sinners were all drawing near to hear Jesus, but the Pharisees and the scribes complained, saying, "This man welcomes sinners and eats with them."

So Jesus told them this parable:

"Suppose one of you is a shepherd with a hundred sheep and loses one of them..."

"Shepherd!" shouted the Pharisees angrily, "None of us would be seen dead in that profession! They're untrustworthy and unclean!"

"But..."

And they stormed off.

2

Suppose one of you has a hundred sheep and loses one of them. Wouldn't he call together his friends and neighbours saying, "Rejoice with me, for I have ninety-nine sheep which is more than any other shepherd around!"

In the same way, there is more joy in heaven over the size of churches rather than over finding the lost.

3

What do you think? If a man has one hundred sheep and one of them goes astray, does he not notice because he's too busy looking at his phone? After all, watching over sheep is mind-numbingly dull.

In the same way, your Father in heaven has far more important things to do than keep tabs on sinners that wander off.

4

Suppose one of you has a hundred sheep and loses one of them. Would he not leave the ninety-nine in the open country and go after the one that is lost until he finds it?"

And when he finds it, he will carry it back to the others in the country. He would hardly call together his friends and neighbours to rejoice with him. After all it's only a stupid sheep.

5

What do you think? If a man has one hundred sheep and one of them goes astray, does he not go searching for the wayward one until he finds it? And when he finds it, doesn't he slaughter it there and then, and then rejoice as he heads home after a job well done?

In the same way there is more joy in heaven over one sinner who is obliterated before God than the ninety-nine righteous people who please God.

6

What do you think? If a man has one hundred sheep would he not put up an electric fence around them and fit each of them with GPS trackers?

For then none shall ever go astray.

In the same way, your Father in heaven is not willing to risk allowing anyone to be free to reject His love.

7

Suppose one of you has a hundred sheep and loses one of them. Wouldn't he stay with the ninety-nine in the open country as the needs of the many outweigh the needs of the one?

And wouldn't the rest of flock take comfort that should they get lost then they too would be sacrificed in the name of the larger good of the group?

In the same way, your Father is more concerned over the ninety-nine rather than any single individual.

8

Suppose one of you has a hundred sheep and loses one of them. Would he not send a servant to go after the one that is lost, while he stays with the ninety-nine in the open country?

In the same way, your almighty and eternal God will not get His hands dirty by actually coming down from heaven to go searching for one sinner.

9

What do you think? If a man has one hundred sheep and one of them goes astray, do not the ninety-nine sheep say things like "I always thought that one was a bit dodgy." or "Yeah, I never thought they were a proper sheep at all."

10

Now the tax collectors and other notorious sinners were all drawing near to hear Jesus, but the Pharisees and the scribes complained, saying, "This man welcomes sinners and eats with them."

So Jesus told them this parable:

"Suppose one of you has a hundred sheep and loses one of them. Wouldn't he leave the ninety-nine in the open country and go after the one that is lost until he finds it?

"And when he finds it, he will joyfully carry it home on his shoulders. When he arrives, he calls together his friends and neighbours saying, 'Rejoice with me, for I have found my sheep that was lost!'"

"In the same way, there is more joy in heaven over one sinner who repents than over ninety-nine righteous people who need no repentance."

But then one of the Pharisees replied, "But surely no one is righteous except God."

Jesus responded, "Precisely."

11

Suppose one of you has a hundred sheep and loses one of them. Wouldn't he leave the ninety-nine in the open country and go after the one that is lost until he finds it?

And when he finds it, will he not leave it there and head home? And when he arrives, he calls together his friends and neighbours saying, "Rejoice with me, for I found my sheep that was lost!"

In the same way, there is joy in heaven over knowing where people are at than actually bringing them home.

12

Suppose one of you has a hundred sheep and loses one of them. Wouldn't he hope it was only a little lamb rather than a fully-grown sheep? And when he discovers that it is not, would he not secretly hope than he finds the animal dead or devoured by a lion so he needs only to gather a few scraps of hide and bone as proof that he neither stole nor sold the beast?

And should he find it alive and well, does he not ride that sheep home rather than face the back-breaking task of carrying it on his shoulders over rough terrain?

In the same way, there is more reluctance in heaven over the arduous task of seeking and finding one sinner than staying in the glory.

13

Suppose one of you has a hundred sheep and loses one of them. Wouldn't he leave the ninety-nine in the open country and go after the one that is lost until he finds it?

And when he finds it, he will joyfully carry it home on his shoulders. When he arrives, he calls together his friends and neighbours saying, "Rejoice with me, for I have found my sheep that was lost!"

And will not his friends and neighbours say, "Why have you left the other ninety-nine in the wilderness instead of bringing them safely home? That's downright irresponsible! Especially since some of those sheep are ours in the communal flock!"

14

What do you think? If a man has one hundred sheep and one of them goes astray, do not the ninety-nine say, "Woohoo! More grass for us! His loss, our gain."

15

Suppose a parent has six children and loses one. Do they not console themselves that they still have five?

16

Suppose one of you has a hundred sheep and loses one of them. Wouldn't he leave the ninety-nine in the open country and go after the one that is lost until he finds it?

And when he finds it, he will joyfully carry it home on his shoulders. When he arrives, he calls together his friends and neighbours saying, "Rejoice with me, for I have found my sheep that was lost!"

And will not his friends and neighbours say, "Why have you left the other ninety-nine in the wilderness instead of also bringing them safely home?" And the shepherd will reply, "Because they didn't want to come and celebrate with me."

17

Suppose one of you has a hundred sheep and receives a report that one was lost, would he not send a servant to the shepherd responsible and threaten him with dismissal if he didn't find the lost sheep?

In the same way, your Father in heaven is more concerned with assigning blame than ensuring one of these little ones should not perish.[1]

---

[1] Taken from Kenneth E Bailey's excellent book, "The Cross and the Prodigal".

18

"What do you think? If a man has one hundred sheep and one of them goes astray, does not the heartache cause him to break down in tears? And does not that heartache lead to his decision to no longer be a shepherd?"

19

Suppose one of you has a hundred sheep and loses one of them. Wouldn't he leave the ninety-nine in the open country and go after the one that is lost until he finds it?

And when he finds it, he will joyfully carry it home on his shoulders. When he arrives, he calls together his friends and neighbours saying, "Rejoice with me, for I have brought dinner!"

In the same way, there is more joy in churches over bringing back one tither than over ninety-nine congregants who don't tithe.

20

What do you think? If a man has one hundred sheep and one of them goes astray, does he not advertise to other shepherd's flocks, telling them how much better his pasture is? And will he not soon gain sheep at the other shepherd's expense? And when he does, will he not rejoice that he has at least 100 sheep yet again?

21

What do you think? If a man has one hundred sheep, do not the people say "This shepherd is exceedingly wealthy?" and do they not demand that the government tax them until they are brought down to their level?

22

Suppose one of you has a hundred sheep and loses one of them. Wouldn't he call together his friends and neighbours saying, "Rejoice with me, for I have ninety-nine sheep that didn't wander off!"

In the same way, there is more joy in heaven over ninety-nine righteous people who need no repentance than one sinner who wanders off but then later repents.

23

What do you think? If a man has one hundred sheep and one of them goes astray, does he not deny all responsibility and say, "It's not my fault that dumb sheep wandered off."

In the same way, your Father in heaven will wash his hands of you if you desert him.

24

Suppose one of you has a hundred sheep and loses one of them. Wouldn't he leave the ninety-nine in the open country and go after the one that is lost until he finds it?

And when he finds it, he carries it back to the other ninety-nine. Job done.

In the same way, your Father in heaven does not let his emotions get the better of him like those Pentecostals. He serenely acknowledges everything working according to His will.

25

Now the tax collectors and other notorious sinners were all drawing near to hear Jesus, but the Pharisees and the scribes complained, saying, "This man welcomes sinners and eats with them."

So, Jesus said to them, "You lost those under your care! I'm going after them and bringing them home. Boy, you have the gall to come to me, complaining! Don't you realise that I am covering for your mistakes?"[2]

---

[2] Taken from Kenneth E Bailey's excellent book, "The Cross and the Prodigal".

Not the Parable of the Lost Sheep

Perfect Parables

What would it be like if all the characters in the parables made the right choices?

42 | Not the Parable of the Lost Sheep

26

Now the tax collectors and other notorious sinners were all drawing near to hear Jesus, and the Pharisees and the scribes rejoiced, saying, "This man welcomes sinners and brings them back to our heavenly Father."

44 | Not the Parable of the Lost Sheep

Pointless Parables

Just for a little light hearted fun...

Not the Parable of the Lost Sheep

27

A man had some sheep. He wasn't quite sure how many he had as he kept falling asleep whenever he tried to count them.

28

A man had one hundred sheep and one of them wandered away. He found it. The end.

29

Suppose one of you has a hundred sheep and loses one of them. Wouldn't he leave the ninety-nine in the open country and go after the one that is lost until he finds it?

But if that sheep realises it is Passover, will it not keep hidden and refuse to be found?

30

A man had a hundred sheep, but one went wandering. As all the other sheep had followed that one, they were easy to find.

31

A man had a hundred sheep however one of them wandered away. But when he rounded them up he had a hundred sheep.

Mathematicians laugh, everyone else looks slightly confused

32

Suppose one of you has a hundred sheep and one of those sheep set off for pastures green elsewhere. However, after a while there was a great famine, and that sheep began to starve.

The sheep finally came to its senses and said, "With the shepherd I'll not want for he makes me lie down in green pastures and here I am in the valley of the shadow of death!"

And so, the sheep got up and headed home to the shepherd. But while it was still a long way off, the shepherd saw the sheep and was filled with compassion. He ran to his sheep, embraced it in his arms, and showered it with kisses; which was a little odd. The sheep began its speech, "Shepherd, I have sinned against God and against you. I am no longer worthy to be a member of your flock... "

But the shepherd cut the sheep off and said, "Quick! Let's celebrate, throw some lamb chops on the baa baa cue. For this sheep of mine was lost and is found." And so, they began to party. However, the sheep was an herbivore, and so it stuck to grass.

33

Suppose one of you has a hundred sheep and loses one of them. Does not his mother say, "Where did you leave it last?" And does he not check his pockets and look behind the sofa?

And when he finds it, does he not say, "I wondered why that cushion was so comfy?"

54 | Not the Parable of the Lost Sheep

Punny Parables

Hear O Israel, the LORD is pun.

Not the Parable of the Lost Sheep

34

Now the tax collectors and other notorious sinners flocked to hear Jesus as they had done for John the Baptist. However, this really got the goat of the e-goat-centric Pharisees and scribes who sought to put him behind baas. They said, "This man welcomes sinners and eats with them."

So Jesus told them this parable to ram some sense into them.

"Stop me if you've herd this one, but there was a shepherd who was outstanding in his field. And he watched over one hundred sheep but still one went astray. He doubled checked by counting but that sheep had sailed.

"A hired hand joked unto him, 'Hay, did it slip pasture eyes saying, 'Catch ewe later?'"

"The other hired hands laughed, 'Baa ha-ha!' Pained, the shepherd complained, 'Manure making some awful puns today.'"

"Seeing how the shepherd looked forlorn, the hired hand sheepishly replied, 'Sheer up. Accidents wool happen.'"

"But the shepherd replied, 'You've goat to be kidding me!

That sheep was ewe-nique! There's no way the boss will find another like her again. He's a sheep skate. Not only that, he was fleeced last time at the auction.'"

"'I confess I've never met herbivore but maybe she'll come to her senses and make a ewe turn…'"

"'Well thanks for mutton!' the shepherd sighed as he set off in search of the lost sheep."

"After a long graze-y day clambering over the inhospitable terrain, by shear force of will he eventually found the sheep alive and wool."

"He joyfully carried it back on his shoulders and the hired hands shouted, 'Three shears for the shepherd! He should get a graze for all his hard work.'"

The LOST Parables

Allegorical tales that speak straight to the heart.

Not the Parable of the Lost Sheep

The parable of the Paraplegics and the Race

In a land not so far away, there was a 100km race that offered a prize of £1million a year for life to anyone who crossed the finishing line.

Now in that land, there were five paraplegics, who knew they could never complete the race on their own by dragging themselves along, and they despaired.

One day, a master Craftsman came along and took pity on them. He handcrafted exquisite custom-made artificial legs for each of them, hoping they would each enter the race and complete it.

The first man was so grateful for his legs and the fact that he could even enter the race that he spent hours standing at the starting line telling the Craftsman how grateful he was. After a while, it became clear that simply being in the race was enough for him. He even shouted to bystanders at the line, telling them how great it was to be in the race. Unfortunately, he never used his new legs to run. Perhaps, he hoped that the finish line would come to him, rather than him having to run to it.

The second man gladly received his legs and set off on the race at a run. He soon fell over and dented the beautiful legs. He was so ashamed of the way he had treated these legs that he took them off and didn't use them again for fear of messing them up further. As he didn't want to let the Craftsman down, he pulled himself along the route with his arms, trying to finish the race. The effort was too much, and he gave up in despair.

The third man was so pleased with his artificial legs that he took great pride in telling everyone how wonderful they were. He soon forgot that they were a gift. Convincing himself that he deserved them, he reasoned that he was clearly born to be a race runner. He asserted that the other paraplegics needed to be better people to earn the right to wear the Craftsman's legs. But in all his strutting he never actually used his legs for the purpose they were made for; running. Eventually his artificial legs seized up because of improper use and he wouldn't have been able to finish the race even if he tried.

The fourth man was so delighted with his gift of legs that he ran flat out for the first 10km, determined to show the Craftsman that he would put them to good use. But the heavy pounding caused the legs to seize up. Running became harder and harder until eventually he found himself unable to move forward except by crawling. "Why is this so hard? These legs used to work great. Why is this happening to me?" After a painful 1km crawl it eventually dawned on him that perhaps he should ask the Craftsman for help. The Craftsman was delighted to be asked and fixed the legs in no time. The man was thrilled that they worked once again. However, he felt that he had let the Craftsman down. And so, he determined he would go even faster by sprinting even harder. However, after only 5km he ended up in exactly the same situation. He called out to the Craftsman yet again who came to his aid. Unfortunately, this pattern continued throughout the race. As a result, he was exhausted, and his race was long and painful.

The final man was so excited with his new legs that he sprinted off down the track fuelled by the joy and the exhilaration of being able to run. But he soon fell over as he was not yet used to the legs nor the art of running with them. He called for the Craftsman, asking him to oil and repair the legs, soon finding they were as good as new. After this had happened a few times, it dawned on him. If he ran with the Craftsman, then he could receive the help and training he needed along the way. He could run the race more efficiently. He would have regular maintenance and tips that he could apply; ensuring his new legs remained in tip-top condition. And so, he asked the Craftsman to accompany him all the way to the finish line. Although his race was long, he learned to run with the wind in his face, experiencing the true joy of racing. He completed the race, stride by stride, with the delighted Craftsman.

N☒T the Beginning

A clever section title that makes it sound like it's more important than 'all the stuff that goes at the end of a book'...

Feedback

If this book has made you think or laugh or both, then it would mean so much to me if you would leave a review on Amazon and Goodreads even if it's only a sentence saying that John needs some serious help.

Hopefully this will cause other people to take pity on me and buy this book out of sympathy.

Many thanks.

Get Bonus Content

As mentioned earlier, you can receive this book free by signing up to my mailing list and, if you stick around, you'll also receive *"Not the Parable of the Rich Fool"*. Twenty satirical takes on this parable not available anywhere else.

www.johnspencerwrites.com/signup

In addition you'll also receive:

- an email every Friday(ish) chock full of the week's memes I put out on social media
- details of the monthly competitions where you can win free signed copies of my books
- notifications of all promotional deals on my books
- opportunities to beta read and receive free review copies
- the satisfaction of making John feel loved and wanted.

Alternatively, if you'd just like to know when I'm releasing new books then feel free to sign up, grab the first freebie, unsubscribe, then follow me on Amazon, Goodreads or BookBub.

Keep in touch

Mailing list – did I mention that you can sign up and receive bonus eBooks/audiobooks? Just thought I'd remind you. You know, just in case.

Amazon, Goodreads and Bookbub

These will let you know when I publish new books.

Social media

I post daily memes at **Not the Bible** on **Facebook, Twitter,** and **Pinterest**. I'm most active on **Twitter** exchanging banter with the rest of the Christian anon gang.

And you're least likely to see my humorous memes on Facebook unless you choose "See First" under the "Liked" menu on my page. If the thought of this makes you sad, then you know what to do.

Web

I blog occasionally at **www.johnspencerwrites.com**

And I write Christian satirical news at **www.saltycee.com**

Other books by the Author

After reading this book you might be tempted to check out my other books to see if they're any better. By the Law of Averages, you're sure to eventually find something that will make you laugh.

If not, then why not think of your purchase as helping keep me off of the streets where my humour could cause some serious harm to innocent bystanders.

Not the Bible Titles

Alternative takes on the original parables to snap us out of our over-familiarity and open our eyes to the truth of the Gospel.

Not the Parables of Jesus

More Not the Parables of Jesus

Not the Parable of the Good Samaritan

Still More Not the Parables of Jesus

Not the Parable of the Rich Fool (subscribers only)

Not the Christmas Story Vol 1 (with devotional)

Christian Parody Titles
Not the Love Dare
Because everyone needs some biblical help to justify their annoying habits to their spouse

Not the Christmas Story: A Comedic Christmas Caper
"Fear not: for, behold, I bring you good tidings of great laughter, which shall be to all purchasers of this book."

Christian Satirical News Titles
The Best of the Salty Cee Vol 1
News Satire more salty than the Dead Sea.

Lost Parable Series
Short allegorical tales available as ebooks with illustrations for the young and the young at heart.

The Donkey and the King

Ana and the Prince

The Princess and the Crocodile

Satirical Self-Publishing titles
Get 1000 readers for your self-published book
Love it or hate it, it's the Marmite of marketing books.

About the Author

John was born at a very young age with his umbilical cord wrapped around his neck. At first, it appeared that no lasting damage had been done, but as he grew it became clear that his sense of humour had been damaged irreparably.

Not even Bible College, counselling, and prayer ministry has been able to rectify things, so John eagerly awaits the new creation where his humour will be perfected.

John also trained as a teacher at Oxford University, but despite this he still refers to himself in the third person. Whilst there, he performed stand-up comedy as part of the Oxford Revue but got tired and has been sitting down at his desk to perform his humour ever since.

So now, when he's not wrestling with work-life balance or literally wrestling with his four children, he's wrestling with writing funny words on a page in his cramped study.

John lives with his family near Oxford, England where daily he wonders how his wife still finds the same jokes funny after more than 20 years of marriage.

www.ingramcontent.com/pod-product-compliance
Lightning Source LLC
Chambersburg PA
CBHW071032080526
44587CB00015B/2586